SOUNDS OF LANGUAGE

readers

SOUNDS
After Dark

By Bill Martin Jr
with Peggy Brogan and
John Archambault

Acknowledgment is made to Betty Jean Mitchell for permission to use her character Noodles © 1981.

Thanks to Linda Ross and Carol Misiaszek for their editorial and production assistance.

ACKNOWLEDGMENTS

"I'm a Little Leaf" by Jonathan Sampson. Copyright © 1991 by Jonathan Sampson. Reprinted by permission.

HAPPINESS Words and Music by Clark Gesner. Copyright © 1965, 1967 by Jeremy Music Inc. All Rights Reserved. Reprinted by permission. HAPPINESS originated in the play *You're a Good Man, Charlie Brown,* a musical entertainment based on the comic strip "PEANUTS" by Charles M. Schulz.

"Foal" by Mary Britton Miller. Copyright Estate of Mary B. Miller. Used by permission of James N. Miller.

CONTENTS

SOUNDS AFTER DARK

THE TEENY TINY WOMAN

a folktale
drawings by
Peter Lippman
lettering by
Ray Barber

Once upon a time
there was
a teeny tiny woman
who lived in
a teeny tiny house.

One day
the teeny tiny woman
put on
her teeny tiny bonnet
and went out of
her teeny tiny house
to take
a teeny tiny walk.
The teeny tiny woman
had only gone
a teeny tiny way
when she came to
a teeny tiny gate.

The teeny tiny woman
opened
the teeny tiny gate
and went into
a teeny tiny graveyard.

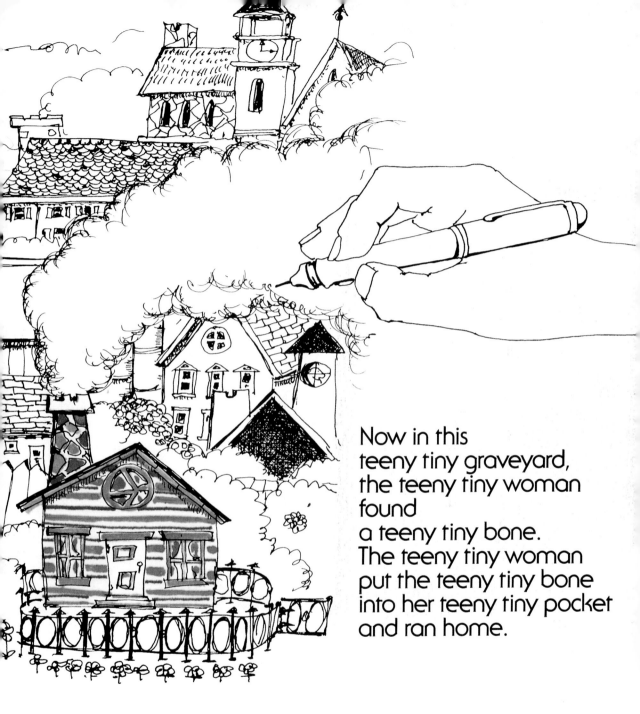

Now in this
teeny tiny graveyard,
the teeny tiny woman
found
a teeny tiny bone.
The teeny tiny woman
put the teeny tiny bone
into her teeny tiny pocket
and ran home.

17

and climbed
the teeny tiny stairs
and got into
her teeny tiny bed.

Then the teeny tiny woman
put the teeny tiny bone
in her teeny tiny cupboard,

The teeny tiny woman
had slept
a teeny tiny time when
she was awakened. A voice was saying:

Give me my bone

The teeny tiny woman
hid her teeny tiny head
under her teeny tiny covers, but the voice spoke again:

21

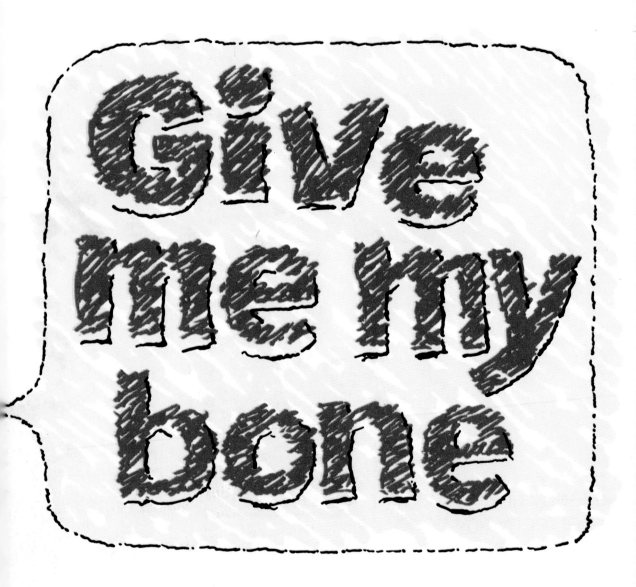

The teeny tiny woman
hid her teeny tiny head
deeper
under her teeny tiny covers, but the voice spoke again:

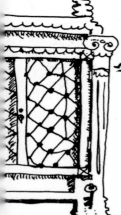

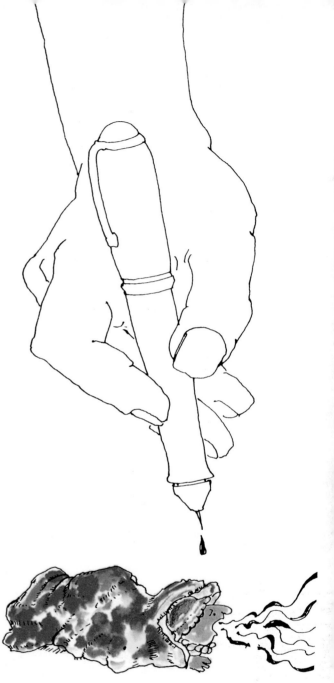

Then
the
teeny
tiny
woman
poked
her
teeny tiny head out from under the covers, and said:

Here is Jonathan's song as he wrote it.

I'm a little leaf sitting
in a tree. ooo what is
going to happan to me?

The wind might blow
me down from my tree.
(cus it has happaned
to a lot of other
leafs you ∧Look !!!
        see.)
I'm changing colors!
Look--red, yellow, and
brown.
Here I go I'm falling
down Wee

eeeeeeeeeeeee

Plunck!!!!

By: Jonathan S.

Here is Jonathan's song in published form.

I'm a Little Leaf

by Jonathan Sampson, 8 years old
picture by Peter Lippman

I'm a little leaf sitting in a tree.
O! O! O! what is going to happen to me?
The wind might blow me down from my tree
'Cause it has happened to a lot of other leaves you see.
Look!!!

    I'm changing colors!
Look!!!

    Red, yellow and brown!
Here I go! I'm falling down . . .
Wee
  e
    e
      e
        e
          e
            e
          e
        e

plunk!!!!

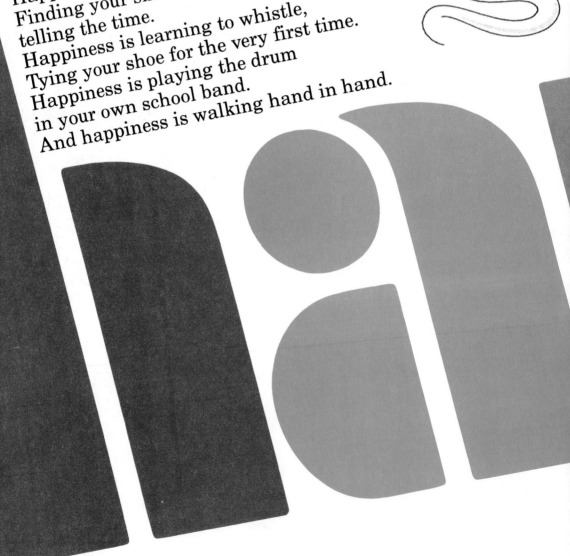

happiness

words and music by Clark Gesner, type design by Donn Matus

Happiness is two kinds of ice cream,
Finding your skate key,
telling the time.
Happiness is learning to whistle,
Tying your shoe for the very first time.
Happiness is playing the drum
in your own school band.
And happiness is walking hand in hand.

Happiness is five diff'rent crayons,
Knowing a secret, climbing a tree.
Happiness is finding a nickel
Catching a firefly, setting him free.
Happiness is being alone ev'ry now and then.
And happiness is coming home again.

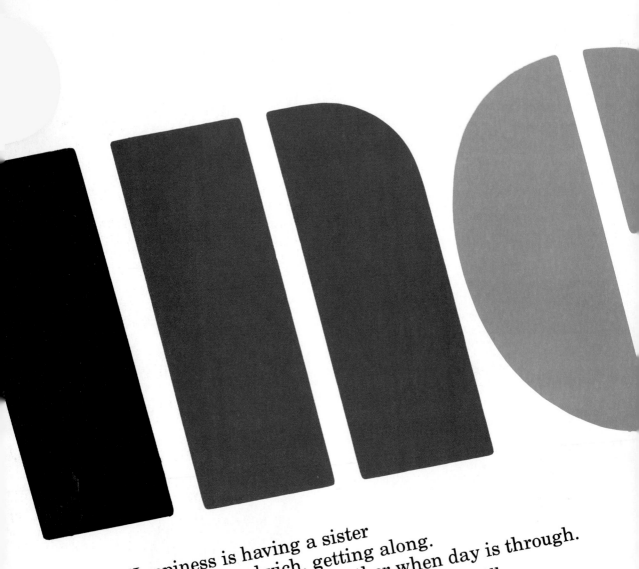

Happiness is having a sister
Sharing a sandwich, getting along.
Happiness is singing together when day is through.
And happiness is those who sing with you.

Happiness is morning and evening
daytime and nighttime too,
For happiness is anyone, and anything at all
that's loved by you.

Foal

Come trotting up
Beside your mother,
Little skinny.

Lay your neck across
Her back, and whinny,
Little foal.

You think you're a horse
Because you can trot—
But you're not.

Your eyes are so wild,
And each leg is as tall
As a pole;

And you're only a skittish
Child, after all,
Little foal.

A POEM BY MARY BRITTON MILLER, WATERCOLOR BY STANLEY M. LONG

Teevee

In the house
of Mr. and Mrs. Spouse
he and she
would watch teevee
and never a word
between them spoken
until the day
the set was broken.

Then "How do you do?"
said he to she,
"I don't believe
that we've met yet.
Spouse is my name.
What's yours?" he asked.

"Why, mine's the same!"
said she to he,
"Do you suppose that we could be—?"

But the set came suddenly right about,
and so they never did find out.

A POEM BY EVE MERRIAM

Ants

One day I found

Upon the ground

A little mound

With ants around,

Running and hurrying,

Busy and scurrying.

I watched them come;

I watched them go;

I laughed at some

That ran to and fro

With a crumb of cake

I gave them to take

Into their mound

Upon the ground.

—Zhenya Gay,
    picture by Ed Young

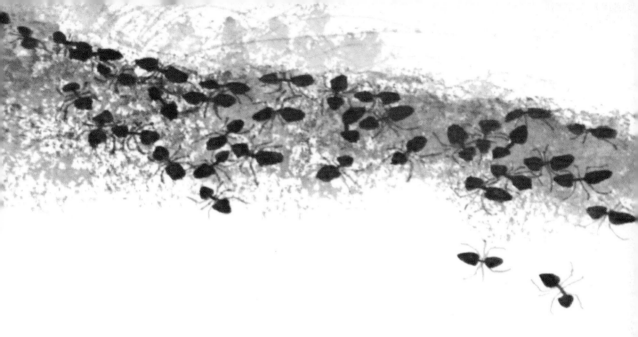

words

ARE LIKE FACES

poem by Edith Baer

pictures by Angelica Lea

words

can be spoken,
printed or penned,
put on a blackboard
    or mailed to a friend,
passed as a secret
    from one to another—
words are what people
    say to each other.

can be plain
    like a loaf of fresh bread,
comforting words
    like your very own bed,
sheltering words
    like the room where you play—
safe, snug and cozy,
    and easy to say.

can be fleet things,
light as a cloud,
lovely to hear
as you say them aloud—
sunlight and rainbow,
snowflake and star—
they glimmer and shimmer
and shine from afar.

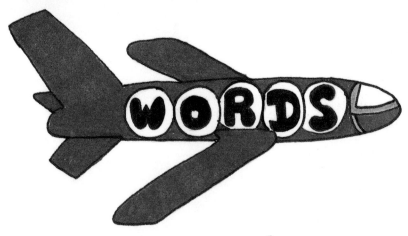

can be arrows
shot from a bow,
piercing and wounding
wherever they go.
Words can be soothing
and healing instead.
Be careful with words,
for they can't be unsaid.

Some words are like faces
    we've known long before,
and some like new places
    to find and explore.
Some twirl on tiptoes,
    some clatter or clink,
and some sound exactly
    the way you would think.

Do you have favorite
 of your own?
Milkshake or magic?
 Old funny bone?
Whippoorwill, daffodil,
 merry-go-round?
Touch them and taste them
 and try on their sound!

43

Words tell you're happy,
    angry or sad,
make you feel better
    when you feel mad,
get off your chest
    what you're trying to hide—

Words tell what people
    feel deep inside.

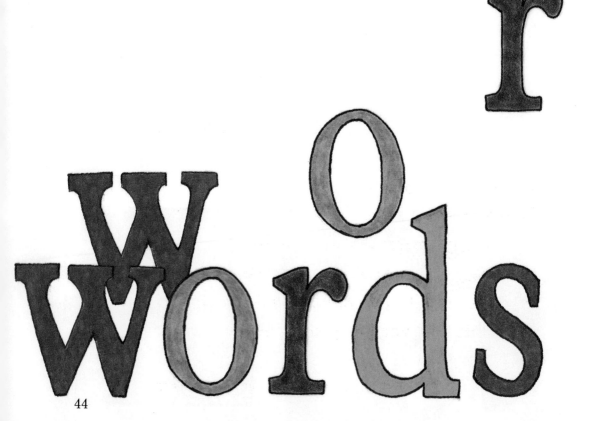

Primer Lesson

Look out how you use proud words.
When you let proud words go,
    it is not easy to call them back.
They wear long boots, hard boots; they walk off proud;
    they can't hear you calling—
Look out how you use proud words.

by Carl Sandburg

KUM BA

KUM BA YAH, MY

KUM BA YAH, MY

KUM BA YAH, MY

OH, LORD, KUM

YAH

LORD, KUM BA YAH!

LORD, KUM BA YAH!

LORD, KUM BA YAH!

BA YAH!

a traditional African folksong
with woodcuts by Eric Carle

Someone's singing, Lord, Kum ba yah!
Someone's singing, Lord, Kum ba yah!
Someone's singing, Lord, Kum ba yah!
Oh, Lord, Kum ba yah!

49

Someone's crying, Lord, Kum ba yah!
Someone's crying, Lord, Kum ba yah!
Someone's crying, Lord, Kum ba yah!
Oh, Lord, Kum ba yah!

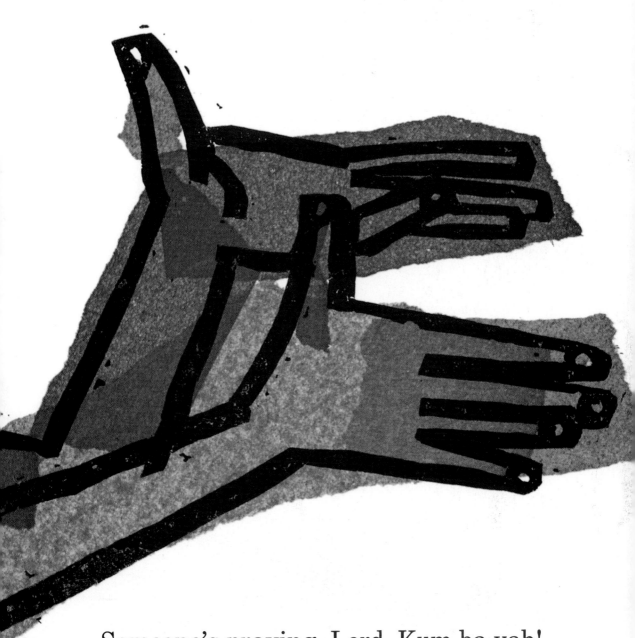

Someone's praying, Lord, Kum ba yah!
Someone's praying, Lord, Kum ba yah!
Someone's praying, Lord, Kum ba yah!
Oh, Lord, Kum ba yah!

Time for bed, the Babysitter Said.

story and pictures
by Peggy Perry Anderson

And Joe said, "No."

54

"Come, come,
you sleepyhead,
it is time
to go to bed."

"Time for bed,"
   the babysitter said.
"No," said Joe.

"I said, time for bed."

"No!"
"No!"
"No!"
"No! No!"

"Let go."

"Get off, I said."

"Get off.
   Get off and go to bed."

Click!

56

"Oh, no!
   Come back here, Joe!"

"Get off!
Get off!
Get off my head!"

Click!

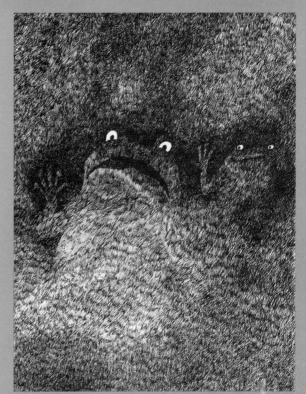

"Come out!
Come out,
wherever you are!"

"I see you in that cookie jar!"

"Time for bed,"
the babysitter said.

"No," said Joe.

"No! No!"

"Please, Joe, please go to bed."

And Joe did.

"Joe, Joe," the babysitter said,
"why, oh why won't you go to bed?"

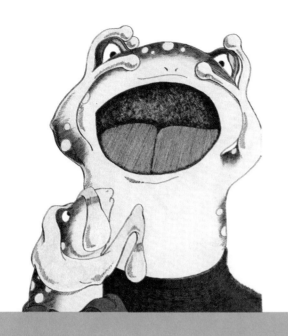

"Because you didn't say please,"
Joe said.

"You forgot to say thank you."

Ten Tom-Toms

author unknown
pictures by Peter Lippman

Ten tom-toms,
Timpani, too,
Ten tall tubas
And an old kazoo.

Ten trombones—
Give them a hand!
The sitting-standing-marching-running
Big Brass Band.

60

Baby's Drinking Song

by James Kirkup
pictures by Peter Lipmann

Sip a little
Sup a little
  From your little
Cup a little
  Sup a little
Sip a little
  Put it to your
Lip a little
  Tip a little
Tap a little
  Not into your
Lap or it'll
  Drip a little
Drop a little
  On the table
Top a little.

pictures by Cornelio Martinez

The Wind by Robert Louis Stevenson

hand lettering by Ray Barber

I saw you toss the kites on high
And blow the birds about the sky;
And all around I heard you pass,
Like ladies' skirts across the grass--
O wind, a-blowing all day long,
O wind, that sings so loud a song!

I saw the different things you did,
But always you yourself you hid.
I felt you push, I heard you call,
I could not see yourself at all--
O wind,
a-blowing all day long,
O wind,
that sings so loud a song!

O you that are so strong and cold,
O blower, are you young or old?
Are you a beast of field and tree,
Or just a stronger child than me?
O wind, a-blowing all day long,
O wind, that sings so loud a song!

Once upon a time there was a boy. He dug some worms and put them

and a pin and a line. and a fish pole.

in a can. He got a basket to put the fish in . . .

The Little Fish That Got Away

by Bernadine Cook,

pictures by Muriel Batherman

handlettering and special effects by Ray Barber

. . . in case he should catch any fish . . . and off he went

fishing. He came to a favorite spot where no one ever

caught any fish. He put a worm on his line and put the line

Then along came A GREAT GREAT BIG FISH

in the water and he waited . . . and waited . . . and waited . . .

It swam around, and around, and around, and around, and around and around, and around and around and around and around.

It looked
at the worm on the pin.
It wiggled its tail.
Then it swam around, and around,
and around, and around, and around and around and around and around . . . right back to where it came from.

So, the little boy waited . . . and waited . . . and waited . . .

Then along came AGREATBIGFiSH

It swam around, and around, and around, and around, and around, and around and around and around and around and around and around.

It looked
at the worm on the pin.
It wiggled its tail.
Then it swam around, and around,
and around, and around, and around and around and around around and around . . . right back to where it came from.

So, the little boy waited . . . and waited . . . and waited . . .

Then along came A BIGFISh

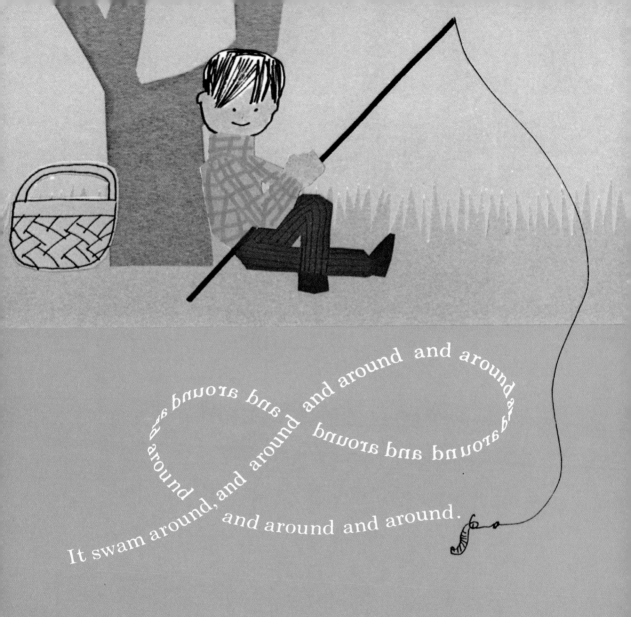

It swam around, and around and around and around
and around and around and around and around
and around and around and around and around.
It swam around, and around and around and around.

It looked
at the worm on the pin.
It wiggled its tail.
Then it swam around, and around,
and around, and around, and around and around
and around and around ... right back to where it came from.

75

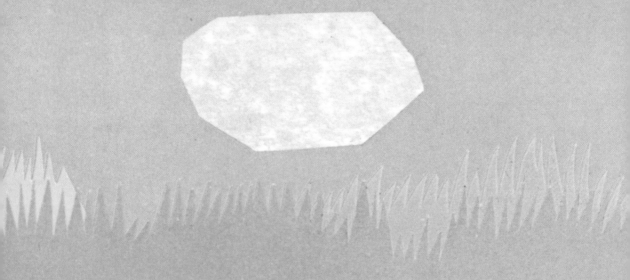

So, the little boy waited . . . and waited . . . and waited . . .

Then along came ALITTLEFISH

It swam around, and around, and around, and around and
around and around and around and around and around and around
and around and around.

It looked
at the worm on the pin.
It wiggled its tail.
Then it swam around, and around,
and around, and around, and around and around
and around and around . . . right back to where it came from.

The poor little boy thought that he wasn't going to

BUT THEGREATGREAT GREAT BIG FISH came back again.

catch any fish that day

It swam around, and around, and around, and around, and around, and around, and around, and around and around and around and around. It looked at the worm on the pin. It waggled its tail.

THEN...
the great great big fish ate the worm.
And the little boy pulled
him out of the water
and put him in a basket
he kept under the tree
in case he should ever catch any fish.

The little boy put another worm on the pin, put the pin

and PRETTY SOON THEGREATBIGFISH came back again.

in the water,

It swam around, and around, and around and around and around and around and around, and around and around.

It looked
at the worm on the pin.
It waggled its tail.

THEN...
the great big fish ate the worm.
And the little boy pulled
him out of the water
and put him in a basket
he kept under the tree
in case he should ever catch any fish.

The little boy put another worm on the pin, put the pin

and PRETTY SOON THE BIGFISH came back again.

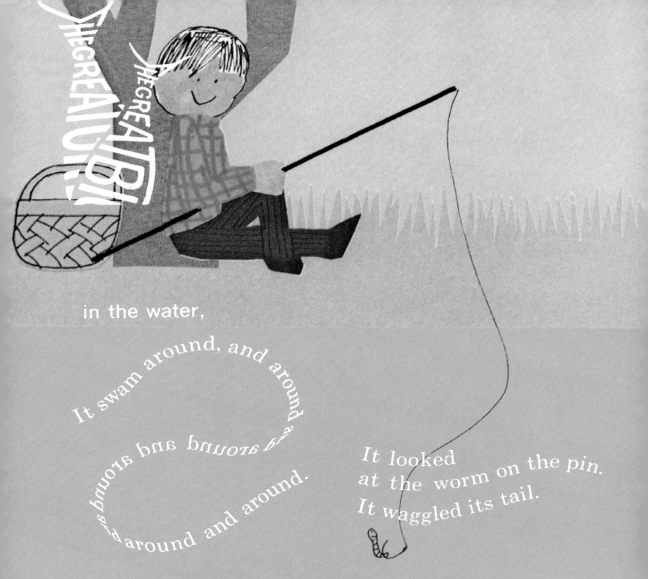

in the water,

It swam around, and around
and around and around
around and around.

It looked
at the worm on the pin.
It waggled its tail.

THEN···
the big fish ate the worm.
And the little boy pulled
him out of the water
and put him in a basket
he kept under the tree
in case he should ever catch any fish.

The little boy put another worm on the pin, put the pin

and PRETTY SOON THE LITTLE FISH came back again.

around . . . right back to where it came from.

in the water,

It swam around, and around, and around and around
It looked
at the worm on the pin.
It waggled its little tail. and around and around.
It sniffed at the worm.
The little boy sat very quiet and thought . . .
hurry up, little fish,
and eat the worm.
Then I will go home
and show Mother and Father
all the fish I caught.
BUT . . .
the little fish did not bite the worm.
It looked and looked.
Then it swam around, and around, and around and
and around and around and around and around and

85

And the little boy laughed right out loud.
Then he picked up his

basket with a great great big fish in it, and the great

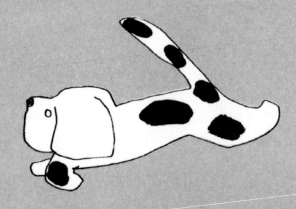

big fish in it, and the big fish in it, and went home.

When he got home he showed his mother and his father the fish. And they were very

happy. They both cleaned the fish and cooked them for supper that night.

His father ate the great big fish. His mother ate the big fish. And the little boy ate the great great big fish and laughed about the little fish that got away.

THEGREATBIGFISH

THEBIGFISH

because he was so hungry. While they were eating, the

little boy told how he caught the fish, and how the little

fish wouldn't eat the worm on the pin...

And they all laughed

THE GREAT BIG FISH

MY DREYDL

I have a little dreydl,
I made it out of clay;
And when it's dry and ready,
Then dreydl I shall play.

Oh dreydl, dreydl, dreydl,
I made it out of clay;
Oh dreydl, dreydl, dreydl,
Now dreydl I shall play.

It has a lovely body,
With legs so short and thin;
And when it is all tired,
It drops and then I win.

Reprinted by permission of Jewish
Education Committee of New York,
arranged by Harry Coopersmith
by S. S. Grossman

Oh dreydl, dreydl, dreydl,
With legs so short and thin;
Oh dreydl, dreydl, dreydl,
It drops and then I win.

My dreydl is always playful,
It loves to dance and spin;
A happy game of dreydl,
Come play, now let's begin.

Oh dreydl, dreydl, dreydl,
It loves to dance and spin.
Oh dreydl, dreydl, dreydl,
Come play, now let's begin.

Autumn Woods

I like the woods
   In autumn
When dry leaves hide the ground,
When the trees are bare
And the wind sweeps by
With a lonesome rushing sound.

I can rustle the leaves
   In autumn
And I can make a bed
In the thick dry leaves
That have fallen
From the bare trees
Overhead.

—James S. Tippett,
picture by Ed Young

TIME

Listen to the clock strike

One

    two

        three,

Up in the tall tower

One

    two

        three.

Hear the hours slowly chime;

Watch the hands descend and climb;

Listen to the sound of time

One

    two

        three.

by Mary Ann Hoberman,
art by Kiyoaki Komoda

Readers' Theatre

Old Bike
and
New Bike

Old Bike: Don't wobble, You've got to keep your balance.

New Bike: I'm trying! I'm trying!

Old Bike: You're less than a day old and already you've got a wobbly front wheel.

New Bike: It wasn't my fault. That stupid dog stood right there and refused to move. I hit him. Ker-plunk!

a story by Noodles and Bill Martin Jr
animations by Peter Lippman

98

Old Bike: Oh, that was funny!

New Bike: No, it wasn't funny! I was doing my best and what happens! I get sprocket shock and a wobbly wheel. That may be funny to you but not to me.

Old Bike: Calm down, little one, calm down. We all went through it. Use your training wheels!

New Bike: Training wheels? Do you know what everybody would say?

New Bike is a tricycle!

New Bike is a tricycle!

Not me! I'm no weirdo!

Old Bike:	What about the new bike next door?
	He uses training wheels.
New Bike:	He's a sissy!
Old Bike:	Then take your knocks and forget it.

New Bike: *(after a pause)* Say, Old Bike, did you hear that kid holler when I dumped him last night? *(he chuckles)* He thought he was killed. The sight of a little bit of blood and he was out of his mind!

Old Bike: Donald is going to take a lot of spills until you get the hang of balancing.

New Bike: He thinks he's so smart! He thinks he has to learn to ride. He can't figure out that it's us bikes that do the learning.

Old Bike: I don't like to bear bad news, but look who's coming!

New Bike: Oh, no! It's Donald's little sister!

Old Bike: Yes, you're going to get a workout. With Donald and his little sister both riding you before you get your balance—you'll be bent and twisted forever.

New Bike: Why don't you take her for a ride? Give me a break.

Old Bike: I'm willing but she likes you. Face up to it! I've had my day. Everybody likes a new bike. She wouldn't ride me.

New Bike: Well, here goes. Wish me luck!

Old Bike: Well, c'est la guerre!

Wild Bird

Round, round, the wild birds fly,
Ka - go - me Ka - go - me,

Poor little bird in a cage, don't cry!
Ka-go-no na-ka-no to - ri - wa,

Hide your eyes and soon you'll be
I - tsu   i - tsu   de - ya - ru?

With the wild birds, flying free.
Yo - a - ke - no   ba - n - ni,

Who's standing back of you, can you say?
Tsu - ru to ka - me to sub - be - ta.

If you guess his name you can fly away!
U - shi - ro - no sho - men____da - re?

a Japanese children's song
picture by Arnold Spilka

104

Hey la la, Ho la, My donkey
and I, Trotting to market with
cheeses and pie, Trotting to
market with cheeses and pie,
we'll never get there, If you should
stumble, we'll never get there,
Hey la la, Ho la, My donkey
and I. Hey la la, Ho la, Oh Donkey
and I, We'll eat those cheeses, And we'll
eat that pie, Hey la la, Ho la,
Hey la la, Ho la, If no one should
buy, we'll eat those cheeses,
If no one should buy.

Oh Donkey take care, If you should
stumble, we'll never get there, Hey la
la, Ho la, Oh Donkey take care, Hey la
la, Ho la, My donkey and I, Hey la, Ho la,
Oh Donkey take care, And we'll eat
those cheeses, And we'll
never get there, Hey la la, Ho la,
My donkey and I, We'll eat
those cheeses,

An old song, author
unknown, painting by
Vic Herman

Hunter on the Horse

HUNTER ON THE HORSE, FOX ON THE RUN, TRAIN LEAVES THE STATION AT **ONE OH ONE**. BUCKLE ON THE BELT, LACE IN THE SHOE, TRAIN LEAVES THE STATION AT **TWO OH TWO**. WORM IN THE GARDEN, APPLE ON THE TREE, TRAIN LEAVES THE STATION AT **THREE OH THREE**. LIGHT ON THE CEILING, RUG ON THE

by Eve Merriam

FLOOR, TRAIN LEAVES
THE STATION AT FOUR
OH FOUR. BERRY ON THE
BUSH, HONEY IN THE
HIVE, TRAIN LEAVES THE
STATION AT FIVE OH
FIVE. SALT IN THE
OCEAN, CLAY IN THE
BRICKS, TRAIN LEAVES
THE STATION AT SIX OH
SIX. SNAKE IN THE
GRASS, ANGEL IN
HEAVEN, TRAIN LEAVES

THE STATION AT SEVEN OH SEVEN. INK IN THE PEN, CHALK ON THE SLATE, TRAIN LEAVES THE STATION AT EIGHT OH EIGHT. SAND IN THE DESERT, COAL IN THE MINE, TRAIN LEAVES THE STATION AT NINE OH NINE. COW IN THE BARN, BEAR IN THE DEN, TRAIN GOT STUCK AT THE STATION AGAIN. Whooooooooooooooooo Whooooooooooooooooo

A PICTURE FOR STORYTELLING
PENCIL DRAWING
BY VICKI REED

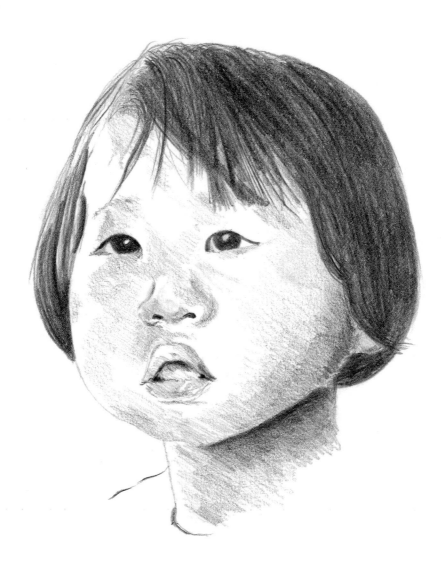

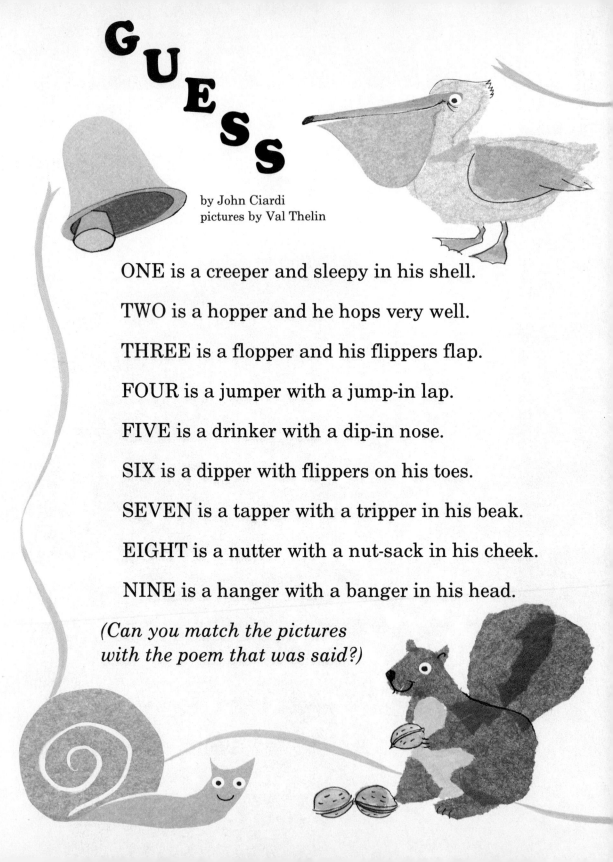

GUESS

by John Ciardi
pictures by Val Thelin

ONE is a creeper and sleepy in his shell.

TWO is a hopper and he hops very well.

THREE is a flopper and his flippers flap.

FOUR is a jumper with a jump-in lap.

FIVE is a drinker with a dip-in nose.

SIX is a dipper with flippers on his toes.

SEVEN is a tapper with a tripper in his beak.

EIGHT is a nutter with a nut-sack in his cheek.

NINE is a hanger with a banger in his head.

*(Can you match the pictures
with the poem that was said?)*

RED SOX
BLUE SOX
WHITE SOX
GREEN SOX
BROWN SOX
BLACK SOX
COLORS·IN·BETWEEN SOX

SOX SONG

by Bill Martin, Jr.
collage by Eric Carle

YELLOW SOX
PURPLE SOX
ORANGE SOX
LEMON SOX
PUMPKIN SOX
MELON SOX
COLORS-SELDOM-SEEN SOX

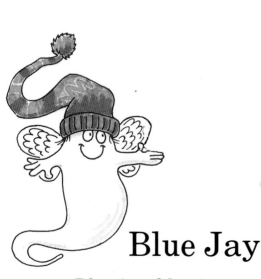

Blue Jay

Blue jay, blue jay,
Out in the snow,
Don't you mind
How the sharp winds blow?

Blue jay, blue jay,
Don't you care
That the grass is gone
And the trees are bare?

Blue jay, blue jay,
Can it be
You stayed to
Keep me company?

A POEM BY LELAND B. JACOBS,
PAINTING BY BERNARD MARTIN

DON'T BE THE LEAF...

if you can be the tree,

by HAL HACKADY

illustrated by
PETER LIPPMAN

hand lettered by
RAY BARBER

Don't be the rain
if you can be the sea,

For the leaf may fall
but the tree remains,
It may never rain at all
but the sea remains,

Better to be the tree and the sea,

See!

Don't be the cloud
  if you can be the sky,
Don't be the feather,
  be the bird and fly,

Clouds roll by
but the sky rolls on,
A bird can fly
with a feather gone,

Better to be
the bird
and the sky
and the tree
and the
deep
blue
sea,

DON'T BE
ANYTHING
LESS
THAN
EVERYTHING
YOU
CAN
BE!

Don't be the sail
   if you can be the boat,
Don't be the lining
   if you can be the coat,

Without a sail
   a boat will float,
A coat without a lining
   is still a coat,
Better to be the boat
   and the coat,

Quote!

Don't be the stick
   if you can be the drum,
Don't be the sugar,
   be the plum, by gum!

Without a stick
   a drum will beat,
Without a sugar coat
   plums are good to eat,

Better to be
        the drum
and the plum
and the boat
and the coat
and the bird
and the sky
and the tree
and the deep blue sea,

130

DON'T BE ANYTHING LESS THAN EVERYTHING YOU CAN BE!

Don't be the string
   if you can be the kite,
Don't be the darkness,
   if you can be the light,

Without a string
   you can fly a kite,
But would anybody here
   fly a kite at night?

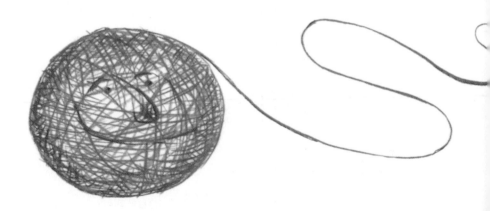

Better to be the kite
        and the light,
                Right!

Don't be the moo
if you can be the cow,
Don't be the furrow,
you can be the plow.

You don't get milk
from a moo, no way!
The furrow's in a rut
but the plow's OK,

Better to be the cow

and the plow
and the kite
and the light
and the drum
and the plum
and the boat
and the coat
and the bird
and the sky
and the tree
and the deep blue sea,

DON'T BE ANYTHING LESS THAN EVERYTHING YOU CAN BE!

Don't be the sting
   if you can be the bee,
Don't be the two
   if you can be the three,

A sting won't get you
   a honey bun,
Take two from three
   and you still have one,
Better to be the bee
   and the three,

Don't be the tail
  if you can be the dog,
Don't be the bump
  if you can be the log,

A dog wags his tail,
    not the tail wags he,
A bump on a log
    isn't much to be,

BETTER TO BE ○ ○ ○

the dog and the log
and the bee and the three

and the cow and the plow
and the kite and the light

and the drum and the plum and the boat and the coat and the

bird and the sky and the tree

and
the
deep
blue
sea,

DON'T BE ANYTHING LESS THAN EVERYTHING YOU CAN BE!

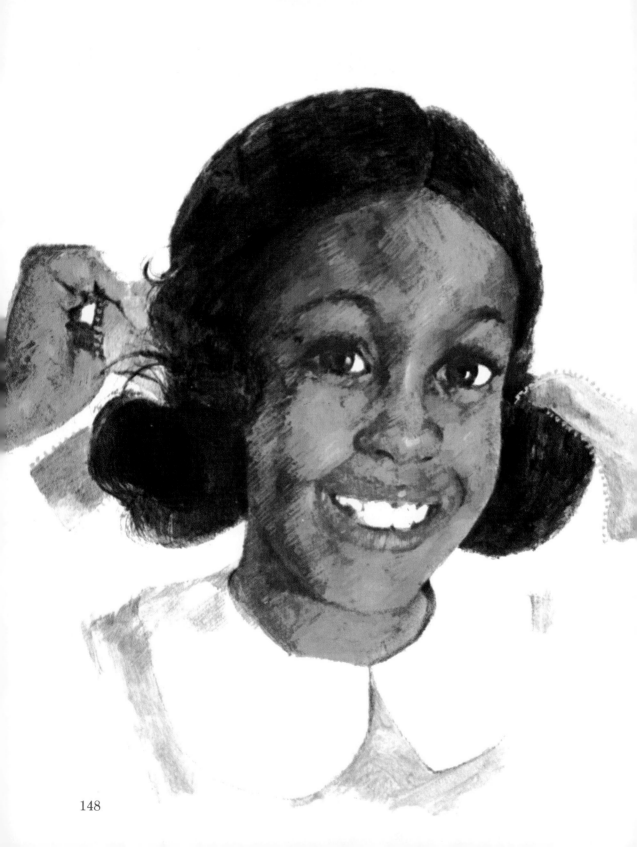

148

It's a Wonderful Thing To Be Me

When I wake up in the morning
and I see a new day dawning,
and I see the sky above me,
and I know somebody loves me,
then I want to stand and shout it,
tell the whole wide world about it,
it's a wonderful thing to be me!

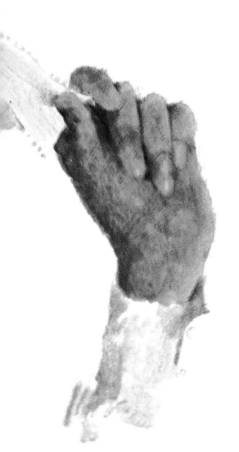

song by Marcy Henchen and Don Besig
picture by Muriel Wood

Once

there was

a man named
Professor Johndear.

He had a wife and two
children. They were
a very agreeable family
except for one great

trouble.

THE MICE
WHO LOVED
WORDS

by Daniel Weiss, illustrations by Dianne Ewell Weiss

The house
the family lived in
had

!.. the sort of unusual mice
that live in professors' houses.

152

They did not eat cheese or flour
or dried peas, or nibble grains of rice
or the ends of spaghetti.

They were not CARNIVOROUS.

They were not HERBIVOROUS.

They were not GRANIVOROUS.

And they were not OMNIVOROUS.

Carnivores eat
MEAT

Omnivores eat
EVERYTHING

Herbivores eat
VEGETABLES

Granivores eat
SEEDS

Professor Johndear said they were VERBIVOROUS,
which means
they ate

WORDS

Mrs. Johndear was unusually kindhearted,
and she did not mind the mice because they
never nibbled in her kitchen.
But Professor Johndear
did not love the mice. In fact,
they made him very angry.
He wrote
a great deal—
schoolbooks, spellers
and so forth—

but the verbivorous mice ate up his best words by the dozens.

Exasperat ing

hee
hee

Exasperating!

Exasperating!

The mice did not eat Professor Johndear's shorter words like **and** and **but** and **to** and **from.** They preferred his words which were long and hard— words like **significant** and **behavior** and **obedience** and **digestible.**

Those mice grew very
plump and bold, and they
took to running out and
nibbling words right
off the paper when his
back was turned.

Professor Johndear
was at his wit's end.

He put salt in the ink,
   but the mice just loved it.
   He tried red hot pepper,
      but the mice ate the words anyway,
   and kept him up all night
   with their sneezing.
   He tried to keep his papers
 in jars, and under water,
and buried,
   but the mice found them every time.

One night Professor Johndear cried out in an unusually loud voice,

'I will teach those mice a lesson!
I will set a snap-trap!'

160

The children heard him
from their favorite spot behind the sofa.
They were horrified.
"Oh, no!" they cried in unison.
"Please don't set a snap-trap!
That would be too cruel!"

"After all my dear," said Mrs. Johndear,
"they are only mice,
and they don't touch anything around the house
but your larger words.
Perhaps if you used smaller words . . ."

Professor Johndear was indignant.
"What? Give up my biggest words
for a handful of squeaking rodents?
Surrender to mice? NEVER!"

The children clung to his coat
and begged him most piteously
not to set a snap-trap.
He had to walk about for a whole hour
with them dangling from his coat tails.
It was very uncomfortable
and threatened to tear his coat.
So finally he gave up.

"I will catch them alive in a wire trap," he said. "Then I will let them loose in the woods."

The children agreed to this. So that night Professor Johndear set a trap, all baited with appetizing words.

In the morning, there were the mice in the wire trap, looking very woebegone. They gazed anxiously out at Professor Johndear.

"Aha!" he said. "Now that I've caught you, I shall be able to write in peace."

Professor Johndear carried the mice
about a mile into the thick woods
that lay near his house.
Then he opened the trap and said, **"Scat!"**
The mice ran off into the woods
and Professor Johndear walked home
with the empty trap.

Weeks passed.
Professor Johndear was very happy.
He wrote and wrote—long, complicated words
with absolutely every letter in them.

But the children missed the mice.

Then just around Christmas time,
when the earth was frozen
and the windows were coated with frost,
a peculiar thing happened.

Professor Johndear went down to the mailbox
and discovered that the newspaper
which used to be called the DAILY BUGLE
was now called the AILY UGLE.

And there were
several Christmas cards wishing the Johndear
family a   ERRY   MAS and a
HAP   NEW   EAR.

"DRAT! It's those mice again!"

exclaimed Professor Johndear.

"They've gotten into the mailbox!"

"THE MICE ARE BACK,"

whispered
the children happily
to one another
behind the sofa.

"The poor things,"

sighed Mrs. Johndear,

"nothing but newspapers and greeting cards to eat, and here it is almost Christmas."

On the last day
before Christmas,
Mrs. Johndear had a great idea.
Without a word to anyone,
she dashed downtown
to do some last minute shopping.

On
Chri
stmas
morning
a large pack
age appeared
among all the
other gifts. "Now
go open the door
for the mice," said
Mrs. Johndear. The
children ran to the door
and called softly, "Here mice,
here mice." Then they went away,
leaving the door open just a crack.

AND THE MICE
CAME BACK

Professor Johndear received,
among other things,
a new typewriter
and a large package of carbon paper.

"Now you can use
the typewriter and your carbon paper
and make extra copies for the mice,"
said Mrs. Johndear to her husband.
"In that way
you and the mice
should both be happy."

And they were.

Here's a Picture to Talk About by Worth Ellsworth

LISTEN TO THE RAIN

by Bill Martin Jr and John Archambault
pictures by James Endicott

Listen to the rain,
the whisper of the rain,
the slow soft sprinkle,
the drip-drop tinkle,
the first wet whisper of the rain.

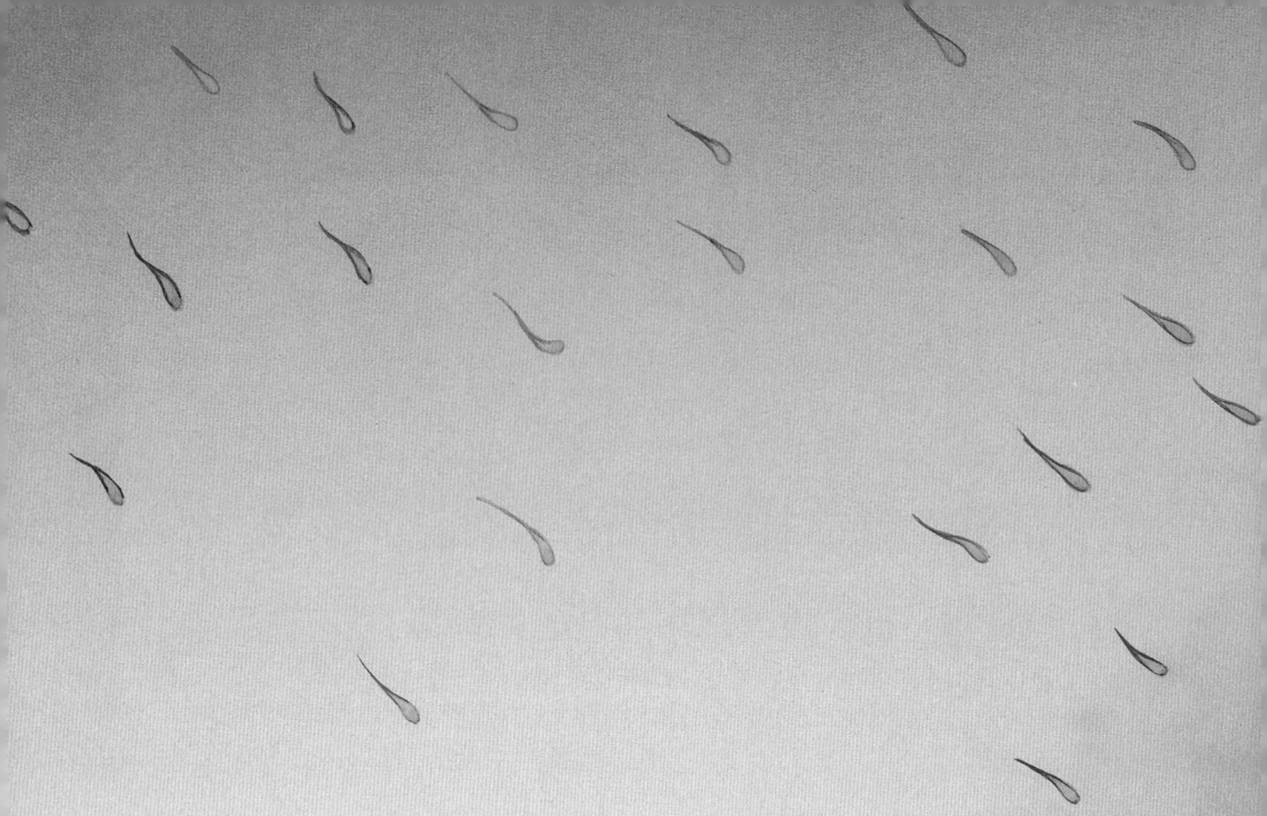

Listen to the rain,
the singing of the rain,
the tiptoe pitter-patter,
the splish and splash and splatter,
the steady sound,
the singing of the rain.

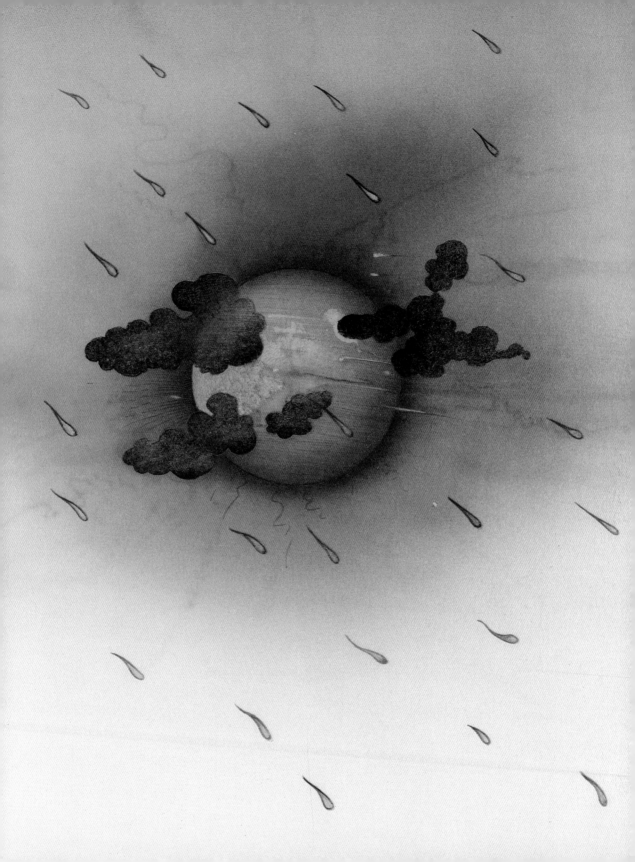

Listen to the rain,
the roaring pouring rain,
the hurly-burly
topsy-turvy
lashing gnashing teeth of rain,
the lightning-flashing
thunder-crashing
sounding pounding roaring rain,
leaving all outdoors a muddle,
a mishy mushy muddy puddle.

Listen to the quietude,
the silence and the solitude
of after-rain,

the dripping, dripping, dropping,
the slowly, slowly stopping
the fresh wet silent
after-time
of rain.

The Owl and the Pussy-Cat

by Edward Lear with pictures by Sal Murdocca

The Owl and the Pussy-cat went to sea
In a beautiful pea-green boat:
They took some honey, and plenty of money
Wrapped up in a five-pound note.
The Owl looked up to the stars above,
And sang to a small guitar,
"O lovely Pussy, O Pussy, my love,
What a beautiful Pussy you are,
You are,
You are!
What a beautiful Pussy you are!"

Pussy said to the Owl, "You elegant fowl,
How charmingly sweet you sing!
Oh! let us be married; too long we have tarried:
But what shall we do for a ring?"
They sailed away, for a year and a day,

To the land where the bong-tree grows;
And there in a wood a Piggy-wig stood,
With a ring at the end of his nose,
His nose,
His nose,
With a ring at the end of his nose.

183

"Dear Pig, are you willing
to sell for one shilling
Your ring?" Said the Piggy, "I will."
So they took it away, and were married next day
By the turkey who lives on the hill.

They dined on mince and slices of quince,

Which they ate with a runcible spoon;

And hand in hand, on the edge of the sand,

They danced by the light of the moon.

The moon,
The moon,
They danced by the light
of the moon.

The Boy Next Door

an old song, author unknown
pictures by Arnold Spilka

The boy next door has a rabbit to sell,
A rabbit to sell, a rabbit to sell,
The boy next door has a rabbit to sell,
I'm thinking that I will buy it.

I've saved my pennies for many a day,
Many a day, many a day,
I've saved my pennies for many a day,
And so I believe I'll buy it.

We'll play together and that will be fun,
That will be fun, that will be fun,
For one white rabbit is better than none,
And so I believe I'll buy it.

The Blind Men
and the Elephant

adapted by Bill Martin Jr
from a poem by John Godfrey Saxe
pictures by Sonia O. Lisker

It was six men of Indostan
(Though all of them were blind)
Who went to see an Elephant
To satisfy the mind.

Against the Elephant's sturdy side
The first blind man did fall,
And cried, "Ah me, the Elephant
Is very like a wall!"

The second feeling of the tusk,
Cried, "Ho! What have we here!
The wonder of an Elephant
Is very like a spear!"

The third took hold the squirming trunk
And very quickly spake:
"I see," quoth he, "the Elephant
Is very like a snake."

The fourth reached out an eager hand,
And felt about the knee.
"'Tis clear enough, the Elephant
Is very like a tree!"

The fifth, who chanced to touch an ear,
Said, "E'en the blindest man
Can see that this Elephant
Is very like a fan."

The sixth seized on the swinging tail
That fell within his scope.
"I see," quoth he, "the Elephant
Is very like a rope."

And so these men of Indostan
Disputed loud and long.
Though each was partly in the right,
They all were in the wrong.

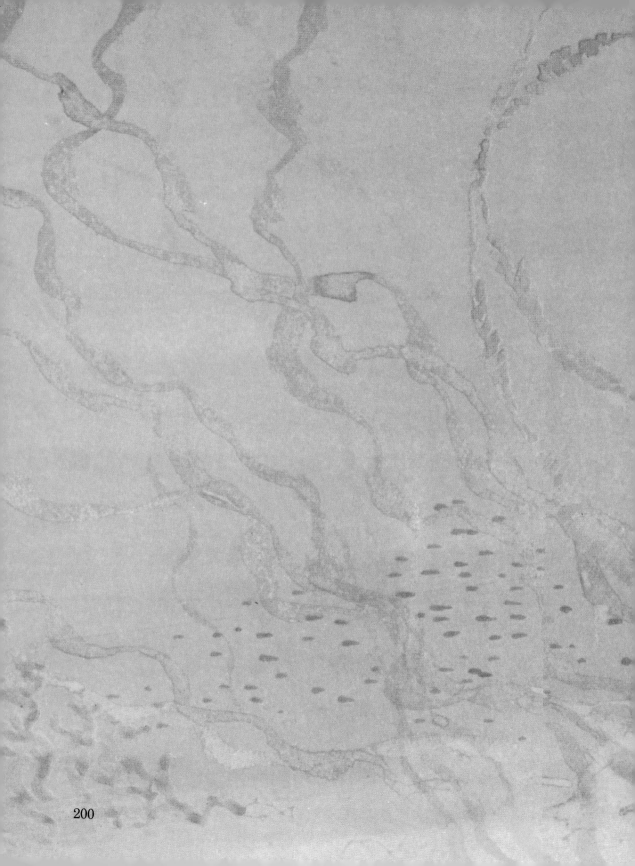

Way Down Deep

Underneath the water
Way down deep
In sand and stones and seaweed
Starfish creep
Snails inch slowly
Oysters sleep
Underneath the water
Way down deep.

Mary Ann Hoberman,
picture by Ed Young

The Difference

Outside
    the world is sky and air
    and trees and flowers everywhere.
But inside
    it is walls and floor
    that lead to outside through a door.

—Myra Cohn Livingston,
picture by Ed Young

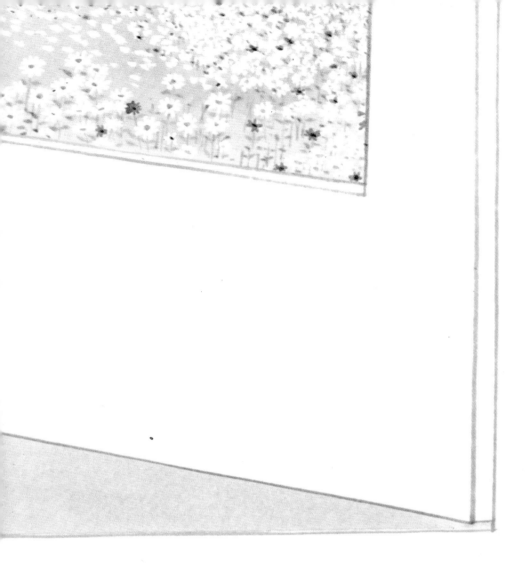

The **Dinosaur** Who Ate, Among Other Things, a **small** Boy

a story by Polly Fox
pictures by Kelly Oechsli

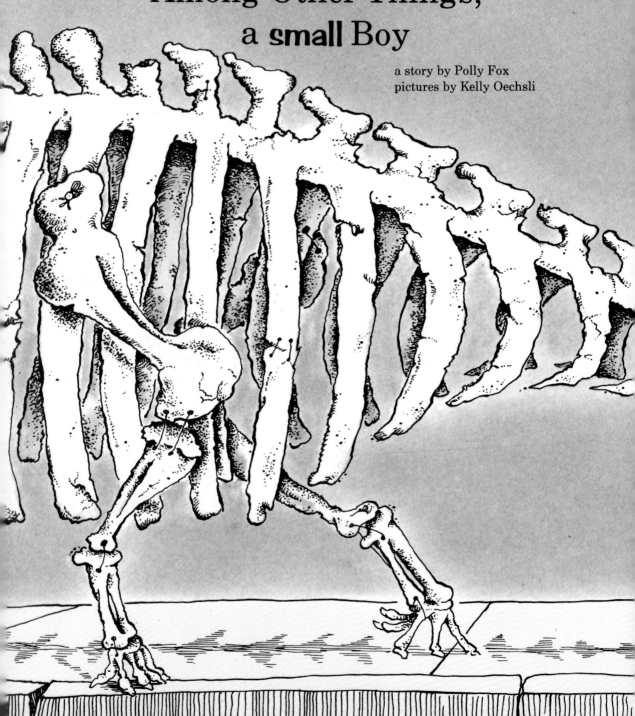

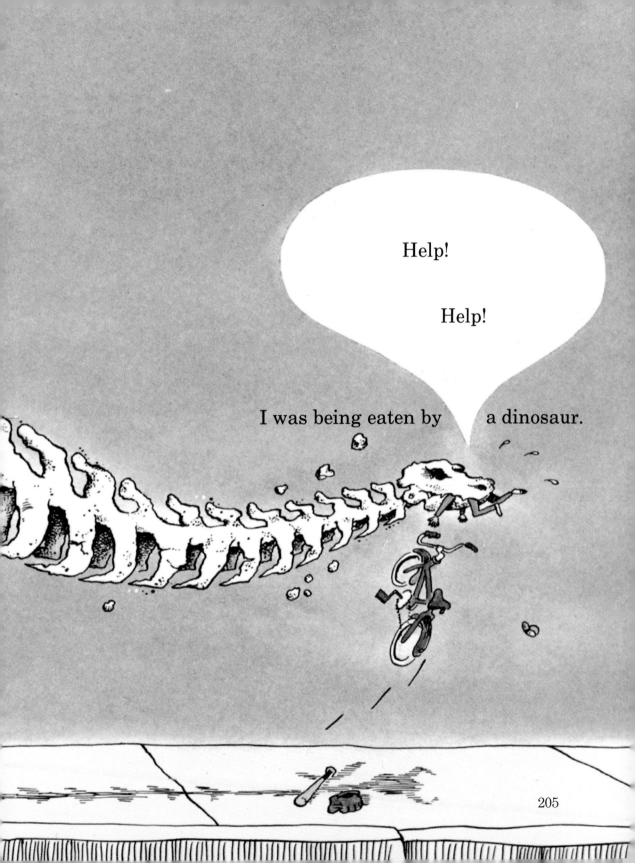

Now, I don't pretend to know
how that skeleton got to Third Avenue,
but I do know that I suddenly found myself
inside the dinosaur's rib cage, looking out.
I wiggled out between two ribs
and dropped to the sidewalk.
"Just who do you think you are,
going around Third Avenue eating people?"

"But I'm hungry," said the dinosaur.
Then to my surprise,
a tear trickled down her long nose
and she added,
"I haven't eaten in ten million years!"

"Oh, you must be very hungry then," I said,
remembering how hungry I get
just between breakfast and lunch.
"But you can't go around eating people."

THIRD AVe

"Then what can I eat?"
          the dinosaur asked weakly.
"Well, what about some leaves?
          Let's go to the park and find some.
          By the way, what's your name?"
"I don't have a name,
          not that I remember,"
          said the huge skeleton
          as she click-clacked along the sidewalk.

"Then I'll call you **Daisy**," I said.

A policeman halted *ttttrrrrrrr*

By now
a crowd of people was watching us fearfully
as we made our way up Third Avenue
and turned over to Central Park.
"Don't worry," I told everybody.
"Daisy won't hurt you.
She's really quite gentle."

to let us cross the street and I led Daisy to

211

a honey locust tree.

"Hmm, this is quite tasty!" Daisy muttered
as she munched a jawful of leaves.
But, oh no!
The leaves slipped right out between her ribs
and fell to the ground.
Daisy was just as empty—and hungry—as ever.

"Here, try this, Daisy," I said,
  handing her an ice cream cone.
"Mmm, delicious!" breathed Daisy,
  but plop! there came the ice cream,
  right through her rib cage.
  Popcorn was no better.
  Neither was a hot dog.
I was bewildered.
  How do you feed a hungry dinosaur
  that can't keep anything in her stomach?

Then, suddenly, Daisy was off with a clatter.

She raced toward a balloon man

over near the merry - go - round.

The balloon man,
seeing a dinosaur coming for him,
took off like a frightened hare,
but the sight of food spurred Daisy on.
She overtook him in less than a block.

215

Snap! She gulped down a red balloon.
Snap! She gulped a yellow one.
Gulp! Snap! Gulp! **Gulp**!
Green! Blue! Pink! Orange!
Pop! Oh, she broke one!
Gulp! Gulp! Gulp!
A cloud of rainbow-colored balloons
slid into her stomach.

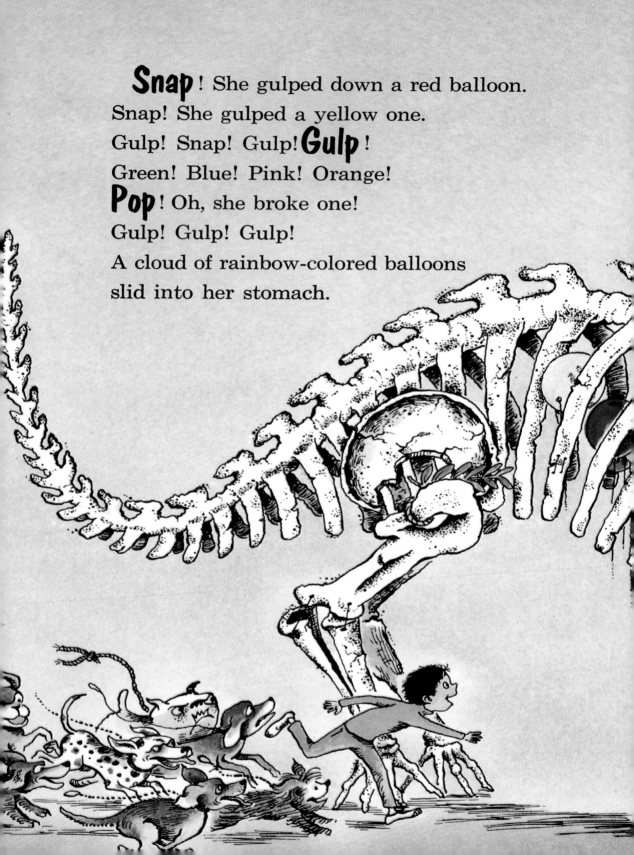

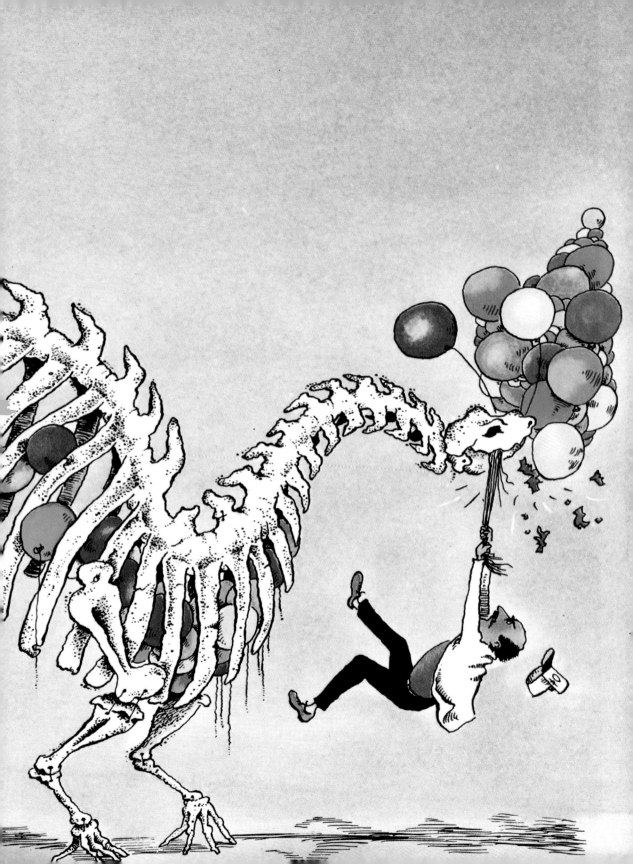

"**Mmmm**," sighed Daisy with a click of her jaws.
"At last! Food that sticks to my ribs!"
The balloons floated about in her rib cage,
filling that big empty space
for the first time in ten million years.
Daisy sighed contentedly.
The balloon man bolted,
screaming for help as he fled.
In a moment he was back with a policeman.
"There, Officer, just like I told you!
There's the monster that stole my balloons.
They're in her stomach, see!"

I dug deep into my pocket
and paid for Daisy's meal.
It took all of my allowance
and my snow-shoveling
money besides,
but it was
worth it.

Daisy was my friend.
I took her back to the museum.

happily

crawled

she

and

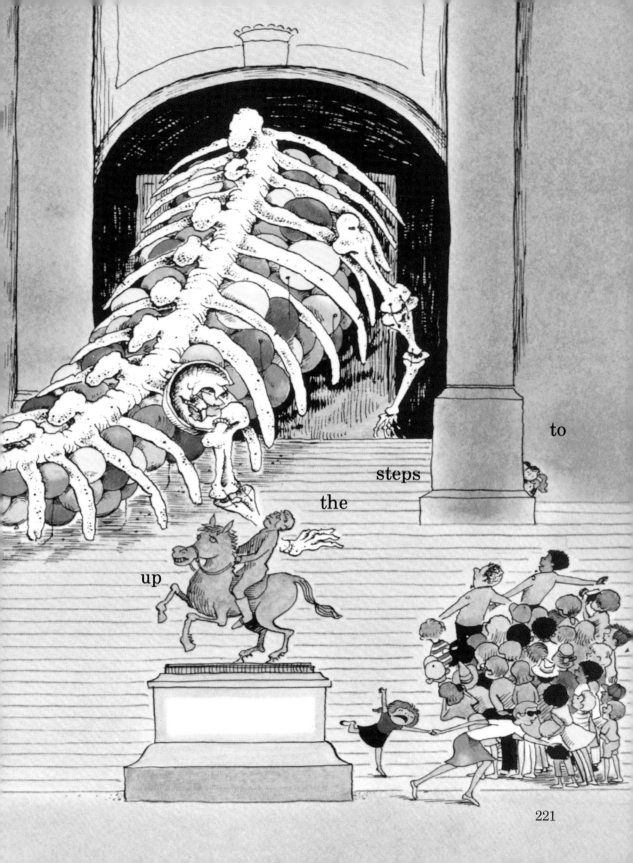

up the steps to

her

pedestal on the third floor.

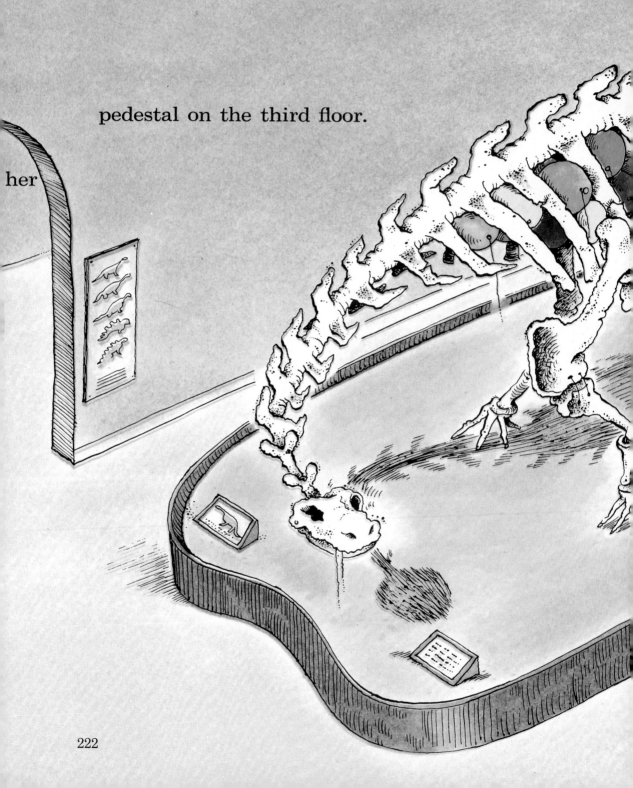

Daisy smiled. She knew she'd never be hungry again.

B - A - BAY
B - E - BE
B - I - **biddy** - BI
B - O - BO
biddy - BI - BO
B - U - BU
biddy - BAY - BE
BI - BO - BU

Hey, it's just a kooky song,
You can sing it too.
Any consonant will work
with A - E - I - O - U.

an old rhyme, author unknown
design by Angelica Lea